NEW VANGUARD • 191

ITALIAN LIGHT TANKS

1919–45

F CAPPELLANO & P P BATTISTELLI ILLUSTRATED BY R CHASEMORE

First published in Great Britain in 2012 by Osprey Publishing,
Midland House, West Way, Botley, Oxford, OX2 0PH, UK
43-01 21st Street, Suite 220B, Long Island City, NY 11101, USA
Email: info@ospreypublishing.com

Osprey Publishing is part of the Osprey Group

A CIP catalog record for this book is available from the British Library

Print ISBN: 978 1 84908 777 3
PDF e-book ISBN: 978 1 84908 778 0
EPUB e-book ISBN: 978 1 78096 459 1

Page layout by: Melissa Orrom Swan, Oxford
Index by Sharon Redmayne
Typeset in Sabon and Myriad Pro
Originated by PDQ Media, Bungay, UK
Printed in China through Worldprint Ltd.

13 14 15 16 10 9 8 7 6 5 4 3 2

ACKNOWLEDGEMENTS

The authors are grateful to Professor Piero Crociani and the series editor, Philip Smith.

AUTHORS' NOTE

In the Italian language male nouns (generally ending in 'o' or 'e') have their plurals by changing the last letter, generally an 'i' (i.e. *divisione, divisioni*); female nouns (ending in 'a') change the last letter in an 'e' (i.e. *compagnia, compagnie*). Nouns like Bersaglieri and Arditi are plural. The basic army commands and units include an army (*armata*), an army corps (*corpo d'armata*), a division (*divisione*), a regiment (*reggimento*) and its equivalent group (*gruppo* or *raggruppamento*), a battalion (*battaglione*), a company (*compagnia*), a platoon (*plotone*) and squad (*squadra*). Cardinal numbers are shown by a ° (with male nouns) or a ª (with female nouns) after the number.

CONTENTS

ITALIAN LIGHT TANKS 1919–45

HISTORICAL BACKGROUND

Italy was a latecomer in the development and employment of armour, a consequence of different factors spanning from the unsuitability of her battlegrounds, mostly located in the mountainous border area, and of a certain lack of interest in the matter, from both the industry and the military. The first step was a request sent in October 1916 to France from the Italian General Staff for a sample of the French Schneider tank; evaluations were undertaken in 1917, while a newly formed 'assault tank office' started to inspect and study the first Allied tank units. These experiences eventually led Fiat, Italy's leading automotive manufacturer, to design and produce a 40-ton tank with a 65mm turret gun and seven hull machine guns; only two of this tank, the Fiat 2000, were produced in 1918, while experiences with the samples, acquired in the meantime, of the French-built Renault FT 17 tank already shifted the attention towards light tanks.

The heavy Fiat 2000, with its bulky dimensions, narrow tracks and excessive weight, was in fact criticized for its lack of mobility and was therefore judged unsuitable for use in the north-eastern border area, where the war against Austria-Hungary and Germany was fought. On the other hand, the French FT 17 tank was considered fully suitable, being lightweight, highly

Rear view of a Fiat 2000, the first Italian tank produced in 1917 and never used in combat, during a demonstration held in April 1919 at Rome's main stadium in the presence of Italy's royal family.

A Renault FT 17 in Italian service. Note the Renault eight-riveted steel-plate turret armed with a single 8mm Hotchkiss machine gun and the three-tone camouflage, inspired by the French one. The officer posing is not related to the tank as he belongs to the Alpini (mountain infantry).

mobile and manoeuvrable. However, repeated requests to France from the Italian General Staff for the supply of an appropriate number of the FT 17 tanks (along with the request addressed to Britain to deploy on the Italian front a 40-tank-strong unit) were eventually rejected, with the consequence that armour were not employed at all on the Italian front and, in the meantime, Italy would start its own tank production. In the summer of 1918 production under licence of the FT 17 was obtained, and Fiat started to develop its own version of the tank, now equipped with a more powerful engine and armed with two machine guns. Delivery was to start from May 1919, but the end of the war in November 1918 came earlier. At this time the Italian tank inventory included one Schneider, two Fiat 2000 and seven FT 17 tanks.

The end of World War I did not stop the production of the licence-built version of the FT 17, even though the crisis of 1919–22 (that saw the rise of Fascism to power) greatly limited it. First built in 1921 and entering service the following year, the Carro d'assalto Fiat 3000 modello 1921 (Fiat 3000 assault tank model 1921) was the first Italian tank to enter mass production, although in a relative way. Far from being the ideal solution, it was nevertheless the only armour available to the Italian army until 1933–35 (apart from some Fiat-Lancia armoured cars), and its assignment to infantry is revealing of the Italian attitude towards armoured warfare during the inter-war years. Although debated, thanks also to a widespread diffusion of Fuller's and Liddell Hart's scripts (partly published in the *Rivista Militare*, the army's official journal), armoured and mechanized warfare were not seriously taken into account by the army staff, inclined only to consider a partial motorization of the army mainly focused on infantry and artillery, and in particular on mountain warfare. Since the Western Desert was not considered suitable either for large-scale offensive operations or for mechanized warfare, mostly because of logistical reasons, the Italian military focused on Italy's northern borders, which, dominated by the Alps, were only suitable for light tanks.

As the Italian Chief of General Staff, Pietro Badoglio, summarized in 1925 for Mussolini, experiences up to that point with the Fiat 3000 tank in mountainous areas, the limitations imposed on tank developments by budget restrictions and the type of terrain where the Italian army was expected to fight not only made the creation of an Italian armoured force quite useless, but also made its eventual absence relatively unimportant to Italy, compared to such countries as France or Germany. Such was the attitude towards armour that in 1928 the budget assigned to it amounted to only 18 million lire, while the budget for infantry was 1 billion plus and that for horse-mounted cavalry, still predominant in the Italian army until 1940–41, was 105 million.

It wasn't until 1929 that the modernization of Italian tanks was started, with the acquisition from the United Kingdom of a light Carden-Loyd Mk VI and a 6-ton medium tank, the former providing the basis for the Carro Veloce modello 29 (fast tank model 29), deemed the most suitable – for Italian needs – tank design for future developments. In fact, inspired by the design of the CV 29, the Ansaldo (one of the leading steel companies) developed and built a 3-ton tankette, eventually entered into service in 1933 as Carro Veloce 33. This was the first Italian tank to enter mass production, forming the backbone of the Italian armour until 1939–40, when production of the first medium tanks was belatedly started. In spite of its conspicuous shortcomings (the tank had no turret and was armed only with machine guns) the CV 33 offered, at least on paper, many advantages and looked suitable for Italian doctrine and strategy. Capable of reaching some 40kph (25mph) on road and of maintaining a decent speed even off road, thanks also to its small size it could move on small mountain tracks and cross every bridge likely to be encountered in such areas. Unsurprisingly, the CV 33 was seen as a fast reconnaissance tank that, on suitable terrain, could cooperate with other arms and perform as a battle tank in all conditions. The fact that these assessments did not take account of tank-versus-tank combat reveals how inadequate Italian tank design and doctrine were, particularly on the eve of World War II.

EARLY TANKS AND UNITS

The Fiat 3000

When development of the Italian version of the FT 17 tank was started in the summer of 1918 the army planned to commission 1,400 units, but the end of the war meant that this was never realized. Eventually in 1919 Fiat developed the project and, with a commission for 100 tanks secured from the army,

The Italian-produced version of the Renault FT 17, the Fiat 3000, incorporated some changes to the original tank, most notably a smaller tail (clearly visible here) and a new armament made of two SIA 6.5mm machine guns. Here the tank is undergoing trials during the early 1920s.

Fiat 3000s of the II battalion, 4th tank regiment training in 1938–39. The tank in the foreground is the company command tank version of the Fiat 3000 B, armed with a 37/40 gun and equipped with a radio and the corresponding frame antennae. In the background is the more common version of the Fiat 3000 B, armed with two 8mm Fiat 35 machine guns.

a prototype was produced in August 1920. Testing was completed the following year, when the Fiat 3000 tank entered into service as the Carro d'assalto (assault tank) model 1921. The Fiat 3000 was not much different from the French FT 17, though smaller and lighter than the latter; it was 3.61 metres (12 feet) long (without the tail), 1.67 (5.5 feet) wide and 2.19 (7 feet) high with a weight of 5.5 tons (the FT 17 was 4.1 metres [13.5 feet] long without the tail, 1.7 [5.5 feet] wide and 2.14 [7 feet] high, weighing 6.5 tons). The 50hp transversally mounted Fiat engine gave it a maximum speed of 21kph (13mph) on road, with a range of 95 kilometres (59 miles). This was an improvement over the FT 17, equipped with a 40hp engine and having a maximum speed of 7.8kph (5mph) and a range of 60 kilometres (37 miles). These performances did not affect, however, the cross-country capabilities of the Fiat 3000, identical to those of the FT 17. Both armour (a maximum of 16mm) and armament also matched those of the FT 17, with the Fiat 3000 having a turret of six riveted steel plates (the same as Renault's version of the FT 17) armed with two 6.5mm SIA machine guns, initially with 2,000 rounds of ammunition but later on increased to 5,760.

The Italian army was never fully satisfied with the Fiat 3000, primarily because of its limited crew of two, its antiquated tracks and its centre of gravity being located at the back, all factors that reduced its use on the battlefield to flat terrain while making it unsuitable for rugged, mountainous ground. Delays in the development of a new and more suitable tank led, however, to the development of an improved version of the Fiat 3000. Developed in 1928–29 it entered service in 1930 as Fiat 3000 B (the older version was renamed Fiat 3000 A), with a total of 52 units built. Modifications included a more powerful 63hp engine (which also led to reshaping the engine deck), and a few units destined for use as company and platoon command tanks armed with a 37/40mm gun. The more powerful engine brought no real improvement to its performance, with an actual reduction of both speed and range.

Further modifications were made on available vehicles in the years to follow; in 1933 longitudinal frames were strengthened, and in 1936 all non-gun-armed units had their 6.5mm SIA machine guns replacement with 8mm Fiat 35 ones. In 1940 the two versions of the tank were renamed L 5/21 and L 5/30, denoting the light tank status, weight and year of service (they were briefly considered medium tanks during November 1938). A few Fiat 3000 were equipped with radios and an external frame antennae for use in support of company and platoon command tanks. Experiments were made on available samples leading to the development of two different versions of a Fiat 3000 smoke-screen layer tank, while in 1932 a flame-thrower prototype version was tested, but with no real success.

The Fiat 3000 was the main and, until 1933, only combat tank available to the Italian army; following the adoption of the light CV 33 tank, it was redesignated as a Carro di rottura (breakthrough tank), intended for use by independent tank units with the task of breaking through the enemy defence lines. Actual combat use was, on the other hand, very limited; in 1926 a Fiat 3000 tank company was employed in Libya against the Arab insurgents, supporting a mobile column heading to seize the oasis of Jarabub. On this occasion the tanks actually slowed down the column, which included such fast-moving elements as cavalry and armoured cars. In 1935 there were 40-odd Fiat 3000 in Libya, used mainly for security duties. With an outdated design and the remaining samples mostly worn out, the Fiat 3000 was no longer deemed suitable for combat and in 1936 it was not deemed suitable for use in the Spanish Civil War. Diffusion of the light CV 33 tank and the availability of the first medium tanks in 1939–40 saw the Fiat 3000 reduced to the role of a second-line light tank, mostly equipping reserve units.

In June 1940, when Italy entered World War II, there still were about 90 Fiat 3000 (now L 5) tanks in use, equipping one single tank battalion in Italy, five companies of the Guardia alla Frontiera (border protection force) on the

A

1: FIAT 3000. COMMAND TANK, 2ND PLATOON OF 2ND TANK COMPANY, II BATTAGLIONE OF REGGIMENTO CARRI ARMATI, ROME 1930

The Fiat 3000 was until 1933–35 the only tank available to the Italian army, and it equipped the five battalions Reggimento Carri Armati formed in 1927. The tank is camouflaged overall sand with large dark-green and brown patches, as in use at the time. The tactical symbol on the turret, denoting a platoon command tank, is accompanied by the numbers painted on the bottom front and side hull plates with the battalion in roman numerals (II) followed by the platoon (2) and an individual (5) tank number. This version of the Fiat 3000 was subsequently redesignated Fiat 3000 A and then L 5/21.

2: L 5/30. XII BATTAGLIONE CARRI L, GRUPPO MOBILE A, SICILY JULY 1943

The L 5/30 (the new designation of the Fiat 3000 B, with a new armament) had its last operational use in July 1943 in Sicily, fighting against the Allies. It equipped, amongst others, the XII Light-Tank Battalion that formed Mobile Group A deployed in defence of western Sicily, destroyed by the American troops at the end of July. Tank is overall sand with dark-green patches and sports the symbol of the first tank of the first platoon, first company.

3: TACTICAL SYMBOLS, 1925–38

The tactical symbols introduced in use in 1925–26 were based on a series of colour-coded geometric figures, with the companies (or squadrons) denoted by having the symbols in red, white, orange, blue, green and black. Company command tanks had a circle, while the three platoon command tanks had a triangle in three different positions. Tanks within the platoons were then marked with a series of bars, one to three to denote the position within the platoon, with the platoon denoted by the position of the bars (horizontal, vertical or diagonal). From 1928 these symbols were reduced to outlines.

1

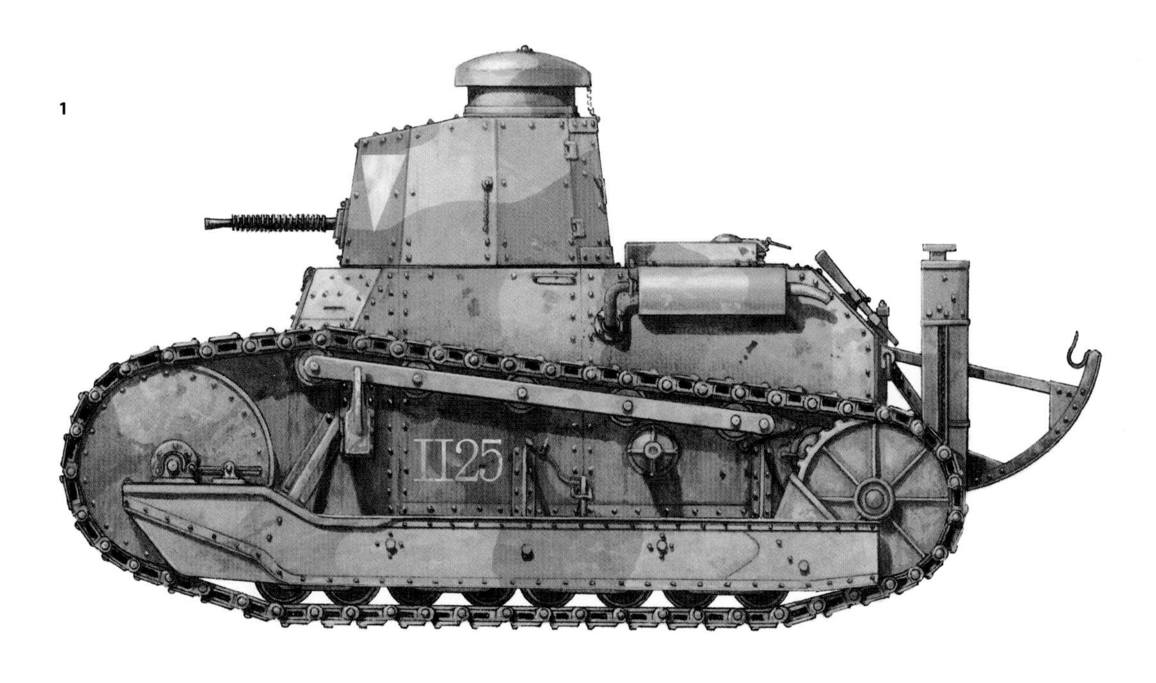

2

3

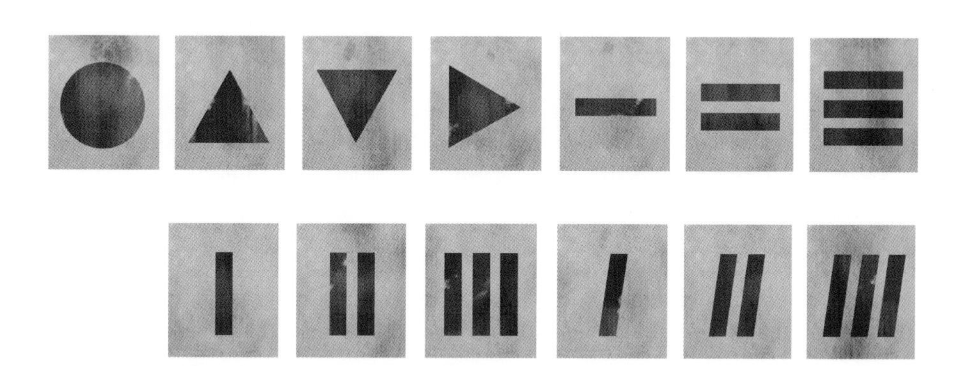

The CV 29 (or Carro Veloce, fast tank) was the Italian designation given to the Carden-Loyd MK VI light tank, 25 of which were bought in 1929. The tank is undergoing trials in the early 1930s.

northern Italian borders and in Albania, and a mixed (along with L 3) tank battalion deployed in the Italian islands in the Aegean. During the war some independent tank companies saw limited use in the Balkans in 1941–43, and in Sicily in 1943. About a dozen Fiat 3000/L 5 tanks were either sold or ceded to friendly governments including the Soviet Union, Denmark, Argentina, Latvia, Spain, Japan, Hungary and Greece. Two went to Albania before its annexation by Italy in 1939, and three to Ethiopia before the Italian attack in 1935.

The CV 29 and the first tank units

In the late 1920s the unsuitability of the Fiat 3000 led the army to start a cooperation with the United Kingdom, considered at the time the most advanced country in the field of armour, and after an Italian mission visit to Britain a sample of the Carden-Loyd MK VI light tank was obtained from the British Army. After some tests carried out in northern Italy, in 1929 the Italian army commissioned 25 samples of the MK VI from Vickers, the last four actually assembled in Italy by the OTO factory, which also re-armed it with the water-cooled, 6.5mm Fiat 1914 machine gun. Named Carro Veloce 29 (fast tank), this light tank had limited dimensions and weight (2.5 metres length, 1.7 wide, 1.28 high for 1.7 tons/8 feet x 5.5 x 4) that made it the most suitable for use in mountainous terrain, perfectly fitting the requirements of the Italian army: a vehicle that could move in the narrow mountain tracks and cross narrow bridges. Initially intended for use in reconnaissance, although the CV 29 provided the basis of the CV 33/L 3 tankette, its actual use by the Italian army was limited to training and experimentation. It was used to re-equip two Ansaldo-Lancia armoured cars companies, meant to reinforce the cavalry divisions, and in 1935 samples equipped with a tracked trailer underwent tests for use as a smoke-screen layer. Renamed L 29 in 1938 (now a light tank), not a single one ever saw operational use and it was no longer in use by June 1940.

The first Italian armoured unit was the 1ª Batteria Autonoma Carri d'Assalto (1st independent assault tank battery), formed in Turin in December 1918 with two sections, including the single Fiat 2000 and the three FT 17 available. The latter were employed in Libya in 1919 supporting the fights against the insurgents in the Misurata area; eventually the battery was transferred to Rome and renamed in 1922 Compagnia Autonoma Carri Armati (independent tank company). Subsequently increased to group level, on 23 January 1923 it formed the Reparto Carri Armati (tank unit), directly subordinated to the army schools for training and experimental purposes. This 286-strong unit was made of an HQ (also including research and training offices), a depot with a repair workshop, and two tank groups each with 24 Fiat 3000, broken down into three squadrons with eight tanks each. Still part of the infantry corps, there were no officers with actual combat experience with tanks, their knowledge almost entirely limited to available manuals. This at a time when Italy also lacked drivers, considering that in 1930 the country only had some 35,000 lorries against the 320,000 of France.

In 1926 the new Undersecretary of War, General Ugo Cavallero (later chief of the General Staff) ordered the creation of a *specialità carrista* (roughly the equivalent of the tank corps), which came into being on 1 October 1927 with the creation of the Reggimento Carri Armati (tank regiment). This was made up of five battalions equipped with the Fiat 3000, each one 100-strong and comprising four companies, each with two combat platoons and a mixed (support) platoon. Companies had an established strength of nine tanks (one company command tank, four tanks for every combat platoon) each, but with every battalion having only 20 tanks the unit was well below its established strength of 180 tanks.

Still, in 1928 tanks were exclusively intended to support infantry with the aim of 'sparing time and losses', specifically breaking through the enemy defences, opening gaps in the barbed wire and suppressing the enemy machine guns. Light tanks, replacing the armoured cars, were also intended to carry out reconnaissance duties in wide open areas but only after a breakthrough had been achieved. Field exercises held in 1927–28 and 1929 sanctioned these concepts, while the 1929 exercises, in which two Fiat 3000 battalions took part, also revealed the inadequacy of available tanks in mountainous terrain and their insufficient armament. Apart from the decision to re-equip, to a limited extent, the Fiat 3000 with a 37mm gun, a new tank started to be developed. This was a fast, light tank based on the model of the CV 29 with the aim of using it in rugged and mountainous terrain, hence the small size as the main requirement.

The early version of the new Carro Veloce, the CV 33 armed with a single 6.5mm Fiat 14 machine gun. Note the pulled-down panel on the upper part of the gun mount and the fully opened driver's vision port, the storage bin and the wood stringer used to replace return rollers, and the internal riveting.

From 1935 the CV 33 was re-armed with twin 8mm Fiat 35 machine guns and developed into the CV 35, a column of which is seen here during training moving past a group of Bersaglieri, light infantry characterized by their cockerel-feathered helmets. Note the tank crews' leather jackets and crash helmets.

THE CV 33 / L 3 TANK AND DERIVATIVES

From the CV 33 to the L 3/35

In 1929 Ansaldo started to develop its own version of a light, fast tank, and the first prototype was produced in the same year. Tests proved the inadequacy of its suspensions and tracks and, following new specifications issued by the army staff in June 1930, a new prototype was built with new suspensions and tracks. Army requirements were in fact greatly limiting, including a 6–9mm-thick armour, height not superior to one metre (3 feet) and width of no more than 1.2 metres (4 feet), for a total weight of 1.7 tons and a top speed of 35kph (22mph). Armament was limited to a single machine gun, with a traverse of at least 30°, and the tank was to be able to tow a tracked trailer. Ansaldo built two other prototypes, including one with an open-topped superstructure, modified suspensions and seven wheels instead of six, followed by four pre-series tanks eventually used for evaluation by the army in 1931, first as an infantry support tank or Carro d'accompagnamento per fanteria. Minor changes were introduced, and in 1932 the tank was redesignated Carro Veloce Ansaldo (Ansaldo fast tank). This was finally accepted in 1933 and an order was placed for a first batch of 240 units, which entered into service the following year with the

B

L 3/35 TANK. I BATTAGLIONE, 32° REGGIMENTO CARRISTI, 132ª DIVISIONE CORAZZATA ARIETE, ITALY 1940

The L 3/35 tankette was Italy's main battle tank until mid-1941, when the medium tanks began to be available in quantity. This tank belonged to the I battalion of the 32nd tank regiment (Reggimento Carristi), part of the 132nd Ariete armoured division as shown by the numbers on the rear plate of the fighting compartment. The new-type tactical symbol on both hull sides, introduced in 1938, denotes the 4th platoon (four white bars) of the 2nd company (blue symbol), with the tank individual number ('2') atop. Licence plates, in metal, were common on Italian tanks until the end of the war. The tank is camouflaged overall dark green, a colour introduced in 1933–35 along with the CV 33-35 tanks, with small patches of dark earth brown added. In 1940 the Ariete armoured division was deployed in Italy and was then sent to Libya in February 1941, following the British offensive that ended at Beda Fomm. The L 3/35 tanks still equipping Ariete's three tank battalions retained their European camouflage (although repainted sand later on), but had the back plate of the engine (with the exception of licence plate, recovery hook and tactical markings) repainted white as a way to make tanks visible during night convoy marches.

2

RoEto

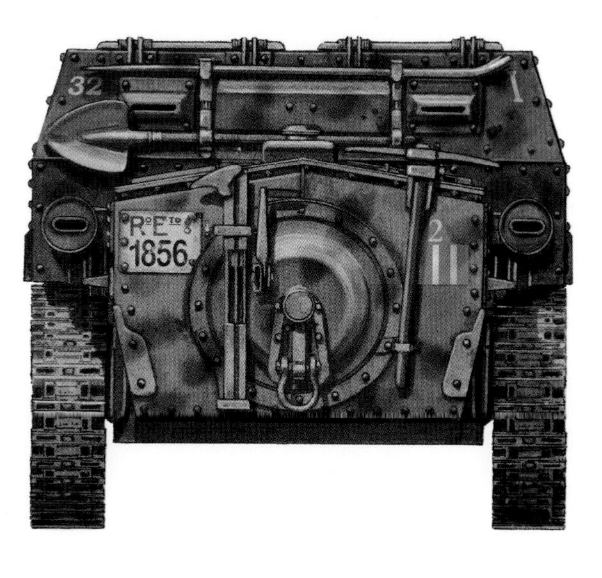
32
1
RoEto
1856
2

The last version of the L 3 tank to be built was the L 3/38, incorporating new suspensions and a different armament, made of two 8mm Breda 38 machine guns. This tank shows the new camouflage, with green mottles on a sand background, and the new tactical symbol of the 2nd tank, 1st platoon, unknown (colour coded) company.

designation of Carro Veloce 33 (fast tank), and were first used to equip three squadrons of the cavalry regiment Cavalleggeri Guide.

The tank, or tankette given the dimensions, armament and lack of a turret, cost at the time 89,890 lire per unit (one British pound roughly equalled 90 lire). Structure comprised a hull, a simple box made of riveted steel plates mostly vertically mounted, with a squared, fixed turret (actually a casemate) mounted on top. It too was made of riveted steel plates, three each side, two in the front and two in the rear, with a limited angle (subsequent production batches also had samples with internal riveting). Internal arrangement had the tank divided in three compartments, with the radiator in the rear followed by the engine and the fighting compartment. In the latter the crew of two was accommodated (machine-gunner/commander, driver) along with the armament, a 6.5mm Fiat 14 aviation machine gun (with 2,240 rounds) mounted on the left side of the turret. Steering levers were on the right side, like the fuel tank carrying 62 litres (13.6 gallons) positioned behind the driver's seat. On the turret roof two large, square hatches opening to the rear were used to access the fighting compartment, while two other square hatches on top of the engine deck were for accessing the engine. External vision was assured by the (relatively) large front vision port for the driver, while two armoured visor slots were located on both sides and on the rear of the turret; with the subsequent production series a removable, aft-sliding plate for improved vision was mounted atop the machine guns on the left side.

The armament, initially a single 6.5mm Fiat 14 machine gun, for which a tripod was carried in an external mount on the engine deck for disassembled use, was improved to two 8mm Fiat 35 machine guns, also retrofitting the earlier CV 33 production series, with the new CV 35 series produced from 1935. By that January 275 units of the CV 33 had been produced, and the army planned to acquire some 1,200 tanks, 200 with special armament, mainly a flame-thrower. Already in 1934 the CV 33 underwent modifications, bringing to the second production series, with slightly modified suspensions, vision ports and slots. In 1935 the CV 35 entered production; shorter than the CV 33, which was 3.2 metres (10.5 feet) long, it had the new, twin 8mm Fiat machine guns armaments, a slightly different turret and, in some cases, bolted instead of riveted plates; 500 units were ordered by the army (now at the increased price of 93,720 lire per unit), and the tank took the official designation of Carro Veloce Ansaldo-Fiat tipo CV 35. The second production series of the CV 35 also added further modifications to the visor port and slots. By 1936 some 2,800 units of the CV 33-35 had been produced.

One of the advantages of the L 3/35 was the ease of transport, which spared them the wear and tear of long marches. Two L 3/35 of the Ariete armoured division are moved on a desert track, one carried on the lorry and the other on the trailer. On the side of the lorry is written: '42° Autoreparto Misto Div.Cor. Ariete' (42nd mixed transport unit Ariete armoured division).

The water-cooled, petrol-fuelled, four-stroke, four vertical cylinder (total displacement of 2,746 cubic centimetres [5 pints] and a normal power of 43hp at 2,400 rpm) SPA type CV 3-005 engine was started using a cranking handle, manoeuvred either from the outside, on the rear of the tank, or from the inside on the rear of the fighting compartment, although the latter was quite a difficult procedure. The front propeller shaft was linked to the clutch and the gearbox, the tank having four forward gears and four lower speeds with the reduction gear. It was steered with two steering and brake levers, and there was also a brake pedal. A 15-sprocket steel sprocket wheel was on the front while the bronze idle wheel was on the back, also used for track adjustment. Suspensions were made of two sprung bogie assemblies on each side, along with one unsprung support wheel on the back between the rearward suspension bogie and the idle wheel. Each bogie assembly had three main, rubber-tyred (like the support wheel) wheels connected by laminated springs, and linked by a longitudinal frame member fastened to the hull sides. There were no return rollers, the tracks being supported by a stringer, made of acacia wood, fastened to the upper sides of the hull. The tracks, 19 centimetres (7.5 inches) wide, were made of 72 main and 72 joining links. Using the steering wheels and the brake pedal the tank could turn on a 3-metre (10 feet) radius. Actual weight varied between 3.2 and 3.5 tons, with a top speed of 42kph (26mph) on road and a range of 150 kilometres (93 miles), reduced to six hours on cross-country. Worth noting, the L 3 tank (its latest designation) could be carried on the back of a lorry (if needed it could even 'jump' out of it) or in a special trailer, which not only increased its actual range but also greatly reduced the wear and tear of covering great distances moving on tracks.

The new armament, two 8mm Fiat 35 machine-guns, was mounted on the new vehicles and also used to retrofit the first production batches of the CV 33. It was operated manually by the commander/machine-gunner, who had at disposal (for the twin 8mm Fiat 35 guns) 2,170 rounds in the compartments on both sides of the turret (later increased to 3,200). Machine-gun mounts enabled a 24° traverse (12° each side) and an elevation of 27°, actually less than required. Dimensions differed from requirements too, with a length of 3.15 metres (10 feet) (3.2 on the CV 33), a width of 1.5 (5 feet) and a height of 1.3 metres (4.3 feet), while the armour was 8.5/9 (first and last batches) mm (0.35in.) thick on the sides and 13.5/15mm (0.5in.) thick on the frontal plates (6mm [0.25in.] on floor, deck and roof).

In 1937 a further modification was experimented with: new suspensions made of two sprung bogies each mounting two larger, spoked wheels (the support wheel was retained), with torsion bar suspension and with stronger tracks. Its eventual adoption in 1938 led to the L 3/38 version, its characteristics almost identical to the L 3/35, although actual production simply came from a factory modification of a certain number of the existing units (as it seems

A nicely preserved sample of a flamethrower L 3/35 'lf' (for 'lanciafiamme) in an Italian barracks, missing the armoured trail used to carry the fuel. Note details of the suspensions and the wood stringer still in place, along with the crash helmet on the top.

200 tanks of this version were in order by June 1940, but only 84 were actually delivered between 1942 and 1943). Also in 1938 a new armament, made of twin 8mm Breda 38 machine guns (with 1,896 rounds), was mounted on both the L 3/35 and the L 3/38. From November 1938 the CV 35 was officially renamed Carro L 3/35, with the L for light tank followed by weight and year.

Variants and derivatives

Several variants of the L 3 tanks were tested, some entering actual production. In 1935 a flamethrower version was produced (with the letters 'lf', for 'lanciafiamme', added), eventually with at least four different models; the first had 520 litres (114 gallons) of fuel carried in a two-wheeled trailer, with the flame projector (range of about 50 metres [164 feet]) replacing one of the two machine guns in the turret. The fuel enabled two minutes-plus of fire, with the actual bursts lasting only a few seconds. A second variant had a cylindrical drum mounted on the engine deck carrying 60 litres (13 gallons) of fuel, with subsequent variants mounting in the same place a smaller, prismatic fuel tank and even a small fuel tank inside the fighting compartment. Although this version was produced in greater numbers than any other variants, as it was intended to equip one platoon of the light tank companies, following its first field employment in Italian Somaliland on 17 April 1936 (during the Italian–Ethiopian war), it soon became clear that the flamethrower tank was not only hard to handle, but also extremely vulnerable. This led to its progressive withdrawal from the front-line use, even though some were used during the Spanish Civil War and World War II in the Balkans and in North Africa, notably against Tobruk in 1941.

Front view of L 3/35 'lf', showing the machine gun to the right of the flamethrower projector and the support for it on the front armoured plate.

A command/radio tank version was also built, officially designated L 3/35 r (for radio), either with or without armament. These, available in a small number, mounted the Marelli RF 3 CV or RF 1 CA radios, and eventually the German Siemens. Only a few examples were produced of two other variants, the L 3/35 *zappatore* (sapper) or *passerella* (platform), in fact a bridge-laying version carrying a scissors

A poorly preserved example of an L 3/38 tank showing the twin 8mm Breda 38 machine guns and the modified suspensions, along with the new mount of the storage bins on the upper portion of the hull, to the front and rear of the fighting compartment. This position was clearly unsuitable, and wartime photos show how the front ones were actually removed.

bridge that enabled light tanks to cross obstacles up to a width of 7 metres (23 feet) (bridge laying horizontally) or a height of 4 metres (13 feet) (bridge laying vertically). The scissors bridge was designed to be laid automatically, and the crew did not need to exit the tank. A L 3/35 recovery vehicle, mounting a towing hook, was also produced in a very small number, apparently (like the bridge-layer version) never to see field use.

Experiments were carried out with the L 3 tanks, including a smoke-layer version with a trailer (never entered production), a remote-controlled demolition tank and the airborne tank, modified to be carried in the ventral bay of a Savoia Marchetti SM 82 trimotor (this was intended to carry light tanks to Italian East Africa, isolated from the mainland following Italy's entry into the war). Neither went beyond the prototype stage, like the Semovente 47/32 su Scafo L 3 (47/32 self-propelled gun on L 3 hull mount), the first – and the least successful – of a series of self-propelled guns produced from existing tank hulls. A version armed with a single, heavy 13.2mm Breda machine gun was also tested but the gun was only mounted on a few examples (that never saw field use), apart from a batch of five tanks sold to Brazil along with a further 18, armed with a pair of Madsen machine guns.

One of the variants of the L 3/35 'lf' carried the fuel in a large drum mounted on the hull deck, instead of using the trail. Although smaller, with 60 litres (13 gallons) of fuel instead of 520 (114), it granted more manoeuvrability to the tank. This is the 2nd tank of the 2nd platoon (see the tactical symbol on the hull) in Ethiopia.

Field modifications proved to be somehow more successful; in 1940–41 some of the L 3 deployed in North Africa were fitted with different weapons in an attempt to improve their effectiveness. The best solution was found by the LXI Battaglione carri L (light tanks battalion), which, between October and December 1940, improved some of its L 3 by fitting them with a 20mm Solothurn anti-tank rifle, with different gun mounts, either on a modified gun plate that replaced the existing one on the machine-gun mount (an unsatisfactory solution since traverse was extremely limited and the handling of the gun inside the fighting compartment was made difficult by the restricted space) or with the anti-tank gun mounted on a frame on the frontal plate of the hull, with the gun breech fastened to

The MIAS (Mitragliatrice d'Assalto, assault machine gun) was a rather odd prototype of a one-man AFV developed in 1935 by Ansaldo; it weighed 470 kilos (almost half a ton), was 1.1 metres (3.6 feet) high and had a maximum speed of 5kph (3.1mph), armed either with two machine guns or a light mortar.

the frontal part of the top of the turret hull. These gun mounts could have a protective shield, but in any case to man them the commander had to open the hatch and stand exposed. Other tanks were fitted with a 45mm Brixia model 35 mortar, also mounted in a frame on the front of the vehicle, often used to fire smoke grenades. Field modifications were extended to the XXI and LXI Battaglione carri L in November 1940, with both the Solothurn anti-tank rifle and the Brixia mortar, and also adding a third field modification that had the twin 8mm machine guns replaced by a single aviation 12.7mm Breda-Safat machine gun (machine-gun mount and plate were modified). These modifications were also introduced in 1941, albeit in a limited number, with the L 3 of the Divisione Corazzata Ariete (Ariete armoured division) after its redeployment to North Africa.

Other than in the Italian army, the L 3 tanks were also used by the Italian police and the Carabinieri (the military police). Several were sold to foreign countries, many being modified either by Ansaldo or by the countries of acquisition; these were: Afghanistan, Austria (which acquired 72 samples of CV 33-35), Bolivia, Brazil (23 CV 35), Bulgaria (14 CV 33), China (about 100 CV 35), Iraq and Yemen. Hungary acquired and produced 104 L 3 under export licence by 1938, while the Spanish army used some of those left behind by the Italians at the end of the civil war. Figures are approximate, but apparently a total of 1,216 were sold to these countries, and during the war Hungary and Germany (from Austrian stocks) supplied a certain number of L 3 tanks to the newly formed Croatian army, while other L 3 tanks (apparently captured by the British) were used by the Greek army. In July 1943 there still were some 700 L 3 in running order in Italy, and immediately after the Italian surrender in September 1943 the Germans captured 148 of them, with some more in the months to follow. These were used (often as tractors) by the German army and others such as the Organization Todt, and some were also used by the army of the German-controlled Repubblica Sociale Italiana, exclusively for security duties and against the partisans. The L 3 tank survived the war, surviving samples being used in the early postwar years by the Italian police.

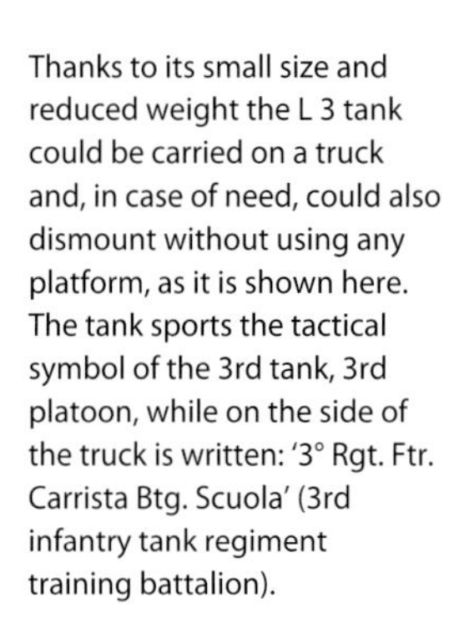

Thanks to its small size and reduced weight the L 3 tank could be carried on a truck and, in case of need, could also dismount without using any platform, as it is shown here. The tank sports the tactical symbol of the 3rd tank, 3rd platoon, while on the side of the truck is written: '3° Rgt. Ftr. Carrista Btg. Scuola' (3rd infantry tank regiment training battalion).

Actual production of the L 3 tanks is difficult to assess, with a total of some 2,000 to 2,800 being produced, export ones included. The overall production figure for the Italian army is set at 1,395, mostly (1,031) produced between 1934 and 1936, although production of the L 3 was continued at a very slow pace until March 1939 (mainly to provide the Ansaldo with some kind of back-up). At the end of 1938 the Italian army had 1,337 L 3 tanks in its inventory, with 1,320 still available in August 1939 and June 1940. On 10 June 1940 there were 820 L 3 tanks in Italy, 324 in Libya, 132 in Albania, and 39 in Italian East Africa, all apparently still in running order the following October.

THE L 6/40 TANK, L 40 SELF-PROPELLED GUN AND DERIVATIVES

The L 6/40 tank

The diffusion of gun-armed tanks and the conspicuous limitations of the CV 33 led Ansaldo to develop a new, improved version of its Carro Veloce. A first attempt was made by mounting a machine-gun-armed turret on the casemate of the CV 33 in the commander/machine-gunner position and, with the hull undergoing no modifications, a new type of suspension was developed with two leaf-spring bogies on each side, each one with two large rubber-tyred wheels and two return rollers. Studies did not go behind the prototype stage of this design, but continued with new models, which retained only the engine compartment and the bottom hull of the CV 33 tank. A new type of suspension was developed with two torsion-bar suspension bogies on each side, this time with smaller rubber-tyred wheels and two return rollers. The larger turret could accommodate a 37/26 gun and two 6.5mm Isotta-Fraschini MGs, one coaxial and one in an anti-aircraft mount. Another version had the turret armed with two machine guns. Results of trials at the Centro Studi della Motorizzazione (centre for motorization studies) were unsatisfactory, mostly because of the excessive height of the centre of gravity of the tank. Another version was therefore developed, this time with the gun in a casemate mount in the hull and a smaller cylindrical turret now armed with two Scotti machine guns. Trials were carried out in April 1936 but this project was discarded too, primarily because of the commander being overburdened (he was to fire both the gun and the machine guns) and the insufficient amount of ammunitions stored.

An L 6/40 put on display at the entrance of an Italian army barrack. Not well preserved, as revealed by rusty stains, it shows the tank suspension and front hull.

Failures led to a step back: the Carro cannone (gun tank) model 1936, a 5-ton turretless tank that mounted the gun in a hull casemate, following the CV 33 design. Interest from the army led to an order for 200 units, apparently premature given the poor performances of the vehicle. The order was cancelled even before the tank went beyond the prototype stage. With the mass-scale production of the CV 33 already running out and the contemporary development of a medium gun-armed tank the urgency to develop a light, gun-armed fast tank became more pressing.

A nicely preserved L 6/40 on display in Turin during an exhibition; note the riveted steel plates and the rear of the fighting compartment, with the protected air intake conveyers, and the shape of the engine deck.

Ansaldo continued its experiments developing the torsion-bar suspensions already tested with the Carro cannone, while in 1938 the army gave its specifications for the new light tank; a weight of about 7 tons, a maximum speed of 35kph (22mph) with a range of 12 hours, a crew of three and the following capabilities: 90cm (3 feet) ford, 80cm (2.6 feet) vertical obstacle and 1.8m (6 feet) trench. The armament, in a turret mount, varied from two 8mm machine guns to one 20mm gun with a coaxial 8mm MG, with the possibility for the machine-gun-armed one to mount a flamethrower in the hull. The first prototype (its hull closely resembling that of the Carro cannone) was submitted by Ansaldo for evaluation in October 1939; it weighed about 6 tons (hence the classification as a medium tank), had a 47hp petrol-fuelled engine with a maximum speed of 34.6kph (21.5mph) and a range of 234 kilometres (145 miles), still with a limited size (length 3.78 [12.4], width 1.92 [6.3] and height 2.03 metres [6.6 feet]). It was armed with two 8mm Breda 38 MGs.

C

1: L 3/35 SOLOTHURN ARMED COMMAND TANK, NORTH AFRICA 1940

Following the supply of 100 20mm Solothurn S18-1100 anti-tank rifles in October 1940 some L 3/35 tanks were modified on the field and rearmed with these, even though the improvement only enabled them to fight against British armoured cars and light tanks, and not against heavy tanks like the Matilda. Only some L 3/35 were modified to mount the gun replacing the machine guns, a solution that greatly limited its traverse and handling, while many others had the AT rifle in an external mount. This is a battalion command tank, as shown by the three colours rectangle, with sand and green stripe camouflage. No other markings are visible.

2: L 3/35 'LANCIAFIAMME' OF 132ND ARIETE ARMOURED DIVISION, LIBYA 1941

The plate reproduces the L 3/35 'lf', or 'lanciafiamme' (flamethrower), on display at the Tank Museum, Bovington, the only preserved sample still with the fuel trailer. Twenty-four of these flamethrower tanks arrived in Libya in February 1941 along with the Ariete armoured division, mostly employed in the unsuccessful attacks against Tobruk in the following April–May. The 520-litre (114.5-gallon), non-armoured wheeled fuel trailer was in fact quite a burden in rugged and difficult terrain, not to mention its extreme vulnerability if the enemy returned fire. The tank, camouflaged in sand with dark-green stripes, has the tactical symbol of the second tank (number on top of the symbol) of the third platoon of the first company.

1

2

An L 6/40 of LXVII Bersaglieri battalion in Russia, summer 1942. The tank in the background has the tactical symbol of the 2nd tank, 5th platoon of 2nd company also shown in another photo. The L 6/40 of this battalion had the tactical symbols painted on front hull, turret sides and rear.

Trials were unsatisfactory, particularly because of the inadequate armament, matching that of the AB 40-41 armoured car. Ansaldo therefore built another, larger prototype with a new armament, a 37/26 gun with a coaxial 8mm machine gun. The tank was radio equipped. A second prototype was then produced, this time mounting the same turret of the AB 41 armoured car, armed with a 20/65 Breda 35 quick-firing gun and an 8mm Breda 38 machine gun. This was successfully tested and eventually approved. The new tank was accepted by the army and was named Carro Leggero L 6/40 after its weight and year of acceptance; production actually started in 1941.

Thanks to its turret gun mount the L 6/40 was a definitive improvement over the L 3, even though it too suffered from several shortcomings. One was the crew of two (driver, commander/gunner), while the tank overall performances and characteristics (limited weight, insufficient armour, poor cross-country capabilities) eventually led to the AB 40-41 armoured cars preferred for armoured reconnaissance. A 6.8-ton tank of small dimensions (length 3.82 [12.5], width 1.86 [6], height 2.17 metres [7 feet]), the L 6/40 had the hull made of riveted steel plates (bolted in the bottom side of the hull), with the upper portion mounting the fighting compartment casemate, made of two plates on the sides and a frontal and rear plate, all with minimal angles. The engine compartment was at the rear, with the fighting and driving compartments separated by a bulkhead. The front hull included a vertical, straight nose plate with a glacis plate connected to the fighting compartment. The turret was made of three plates on both sides and the rear and frontal plate, mounted on the left top of the fighting compartment. The turret roof was made of two plates, with a large access hatch for the commander/gunner and another one on the back of the turret used to remove weapons. The driver, sitting to the right of the vehicle, had a large access hatch on the right plate of the

An L 6/40 of LXVII Bersaglieri battalion on the Eastern Front in 1942; this side view shows clearly the access hatch for the driver on the hull side and the small dimensions of the tank. Note the cockerel feathers on the driver's crash helmet and the straw used for camouflage.

An L 6/40 of LXVII Bersaglieri battalion at full speed on the Eastern Front. The tanks all had the standard camouflage of the time, overall sand, and were smeared with mud in an attempt to increase the effect.

casemate. Armour was 30mm (1.2in.) thick on the front plates (40 [1.6] on gun mantlet), 14.5mm [0.6in.] on the sides and 6mm [0.25in.] thick on floor, deck and roof (hull and turret).

Armament included a 20mm Breda 35 quick-firing gun (normally used for anti-aircraft fire) and a coaxial 8mm Breda 38 machine gun, both handled manually by the commander/gunner; ammunitions (carried in the fighting compartment) included in the latter versions 312 rounds for the 20mm gun and 1,560 for the 8mm MG. The commander/gunner had at his disposal a telescopic sight and a periscope, plus two armoured vision slots on the turret side. The driver had, apart from the armoured vision port, a periscope right above it and an armoured vision slot on the hull access hatch. To the rear of the fighting compartment two protected air-intake conveyers for ventilation were installed.

The 70hp petrol-fuelled, water-cooled four pistons SPA 18 VT had an electric starter with magneto ignition (retaining the cranking start handle), with the two fuel tanks (200 litres [44 gallons]) positioned on both sides of the engine and a semicircular radiator to form a ring around the ventilator, cooling assured by a centrifugal pump. The gearbox enabled four forward and one reverse gear, plus the four forward and one reverse lower speeds enabled by the reduction gear. The tank had on each side a 16-sprocket steel sprocket front wheel and an idle wheel on the back (also for track adjustment), with two torsion bar suspension double bogie wheel assemblies, each rubber-tyred wheel sprung by a curved cantilever with hydraulic shock absorbers. There were three return rollers, the last one part of the suspension bogie. Tracks, 26cm (10in.) wide, were made of 88 single links. The tank had a maximum speed of 42kph (26mph) on road and 25kph (15.5mph) off road, with a range of 200 kilometres (124 miles) on road and 85 (53) off road. A Marelli RF 1 CA radio set was standard equipment.

The Semovente L 40 was the self-propelled version of the L 6/40 tank, mounting a 47/32 mm anti-tank gun in an open casemate. Note the rail on the side, where the crewman has his left hand, used to mount a removable canvas shield to cover the hull top.

A Semovente L 40 in Tunisia in 1942–43; the vehicle is painted overall sand and the crew used some foliage to camouflage it, a common practice in this theatre. Note the crew members, wearing steel helmets and infantry uniforms.

The Semovente L 40 da 47/32 and derivatives

Actual production of the L 6/40 was quite a problem, with the Terni steelworks supplying the armour plates and the engine built by Fiat, also assembling the tank in its Turin works. Production of the L 6/40 started in 1941 following an order for 583 units, the first entering service in May. With the L 6/40 soon showing performances inferior to those of the AB 40-41 armoured cars (in particular poor cross-country capabilities, the tracks sinking in soft ground), later in 1941 the army curtailed the initial order to 283 units, the remaining 300 to be built in the modified, self-propelled gun version Semovente L 40 da 47/32. Based on the chassis of the L 6/40, it retained most of the basic characteristics of the tank, including the engine, with minimal differences: height 1.69 metres (5.5 feet), frontal armour maximum 30mm (1.2in.), weight 6.5 tons. This last was mostly due to heavier weapons, ammunition storage and increased crew.

This self-propelled gun was armed with the Breda 47mm 32 L gun, the standard Italian anti-tank gun. With a muzzle speed of 630m/s (0.4 miles/second) for a 1.5kg (3.3lb) armour-piercing shell (250m/s [0.15 miles/second] for a 2.5kg [5.5lb] HE shell), it could deal with most of the light and medium tanks of 1941, but by the time the Semovente L 40 saw field use in 1942 it was largely outdated. It had a different front armour plate mounted on the fighting compartment casemate, with a shaped protective armour shield on top (the access hatch on the right side was fastened in the mid-series production, and removed in the last one). The gun mount, to the left of the tank, was in a forward position, which hampered the driver's visibility. The gun had a 27° traverse and –12° and +20° elevation. The first prototype of the Semovente L 40, tested in May 1941, had

D

L 6/40 TANK. 18° RECO, LXVII BATTAGLIONE BERSAGLIERI CORAZZATO, 3ª DIVISIONE CELERE, EASTERN FRONT 1942

Formed in 1942 from cavalry regiments and from the 18th Bersaglieri regiment, the Raggruppamenti Esploranti Corazzati (armoured reconnaissance group) filled a noticeable gap in the Italian mechanized forces – that of armoured reconnaissance, a role that so far had been only partially fulfilled by armoured cars. The new RECo were composed of a mixture of armoured cars, L 6/40 light tanks and light self-propelled guns, the Semovente L 40. The three battalions of 18th RECo were split, with the LXVII armoured Bersaglieri battalion being detached to the 3rd cavalry division in Russia. The L 6/40 on the Eastern Front were camouflaged overall sand, although locally crews added mud patches along with foliage or straw to increase camouflage. LXVII Bersaglieri battalion's L 6/40 tanks used large tactical symbols painted on the rear and sides of the turret (in this case the black rectangle denotes a tank belonging to the HQ company of the battalion), as well as on the hull front. The tank of the battalion commander sported on its radio antennae the red fez of the Bersaglieri, along with an Italian national flag and the yellow flag with a skull used by German engineers to mark minefields. Licence plates were painted on the front and metal on the rear.

4062

Front view of a Trasporto munizioni per semoventi da 90/53, built on the chassis of the Semovente L 40 and used as an ammunition carrier (also with a trailer). Note the 8mm Breda 38 machine gun in an anti-aircraft mount.

an armoured turret roof and a crew of two; modifications included an open top (protected by a sliding waterproofed canvas) and a crew of three (driver, loader, commander/gunner).

Ammunition included 70 rounds for the 47/32 gun, close defence assured by individual automatic weapons. This was an increase from the 47 of the first variant, though the radio-equipped (Marelli RF 1 CA) platoon command tank was back to the same number. The 47/32 gun was replaced by an 8mm Breda 38 machine gun mounted in a fake gun-shaped barrel in the company command tank version, equipped with both the RF 1 CA and RF 2 CA Marelli radio sets. The last variant, similar to the platoon command tank, included an external mount for a telescopic sight and an extra 24 rounds.

In December 1941 a flamethrower version of the L 6/40 was produced in a small quantity, the flamethrower's tube replacing the 20mm gun (the tank had an internal 200-litre (44-gallon) fuel tank), while a command tank version (with RF 1 CA and RF 2 CA Marelli radio sets) was produced as battalion command tank. In spring 1942 30 of the L 6/40 were converted into the Trasporto munizioni per semoventi da 90/53 (ammunition carrier for the 90/53 SP gun), simply by removing the turret and the fighting compartment roof and rearranging the inside of the fighting compartment to carry 24–26 rounds (plus some other 40 in a trailer) for the 90/53 gun. Also in December 1941 a L 6/40 chassis-based prototype of an armoured personnel/ammunition carrier was produced, with a reshaped frontal armour plate and re-equipped with the 88hp Fiat ABM 1 engine, the same as in the AB 40-41 armoured car. Known as CVB 5 or Cingoletta Ansaldo L 6 (caterpillar tractor) it had a crew of four and was armed with an 8mm Breda 38 machine gun. A subsequent prototype mounted a Marelli RF 1 CA radio set and a 13.2mm Breda machine gun, with a crew of three and two external machine-gun mounts. Neither went beyond the stage of prototype, like the Cingoletta (caterpillar tractor) derived from the last production batch of the L 6/40.

Thirty Semovente L 40 were converted in spring 1942 for use as ammunition carriers for the heavy Semovente M 41 mounting a 90/53mm gun on the rear of a medium M 41 tank (here seen in background). Ammunition was stowed inside the fighting compartment and accessed from the sides.

In spite of curtailed orders, some 402 L 6/40 tanks and 282 Semovente L 40 were produced up to May 1943. Of these, no fewer than 106 L 6/40 and 86 L 40 were captured by the Germans after the Italian surrender, with other 15 L 6/40 and 117 'Semovente L 40' (all variants) produced in 1943–44 (many handed over to the Croatian army). The last samples of the L 6/40 were used in the early postwar years by the Italian police.

THE INTERWAR YEARS

Ethiopia and the Spanish Civil War

From 1933 the CV 33 tanks were issued to, in addition to the Reggimento Carri Armati, a squadron of the 19th cavalry regiment Cavalleggeri Guide, providing thus the basis of a temporary mechanization of the Italian cavalry. Others followed between 1934 and 1936, with the CV 33-35 equipping three gruppi squadroni (squadron groups, equivalent to battalions) of the cavalry divisions, and the fast-tank squadrons of nine other cavalry regiments. In 1935, facing the impending Italian attack against Ethiopia, the Guide regiment formed nine CV 33-35 tank companies and two groups (IV and V), eventually assigned to the Italian East African colonies. In September 1935 the Reggimento Carri Armati also formed four tank battalions (XX to XXIII), sent to Eritrea, plus one special squadron sent to Italian Somaliland, while another tank battalion (XXXII) was sent to Libya.

The Italian attack against Ethiopia, which started in October 1935, was a baptism of fire for the CV 35 that highlighted its shortcomings. The rugged, mountainous terrain of the region led to a fragmented use of both IV and V cavalry groups and of the XX battalion, which were often employed in rear areas for security duties. The 10th squadron of the IV group faced a serious setback on the night of 14/15 December 1935 at Dembeguina, when its eight tanks still in running order intervened (without infantry support) to rescue a supply column, only to fall victim to an ambush themselves. Tanks were immobilized by broken or lost tracks and by lack of fuel, with the crews forced to exit them either to refuel or to communicate. As a result all the tanks were lost, and only four of the crews made their way back to friendly lines. This accident led to a more cautious employment of the tanks, now mostly supporting the infantry or carrying out reconnaissances in depth. In March 1936 the IV group was disbanded, its remnants absorbed by the V, while the XX battalion (with 12 flamethrower tanks) advanced for 700 kilometres (435 miles) before being transferred to Somaliland. Only a ten-tank squadron supported the 600-kilometre (373-mile) march to Addis Ababa, seized on 5 May 1936 when the campaign came officially to its end.

The CV 35 suffered another setback in Italian Somaliland on 11 November 1935 at Hamanlei, when a column with five armoured cars and 11 truck-borne tanks fought against the rearguards of an Ethiopian column armed with light artillery and armoured trucks; the latter took advantage of the terrain to hide and attack the Italian column and, though the Italian reaction eventually put the Ethiopians to flight, severe losses were

CV 35 tanks were used for the first time in combat during the Italian–Ethiopian war of 1935–36 without providing any definitive test given their alternating performances, although clearly showing their main deficiencies.

A column of CV 33-35 of the Gruppo Carri Veloci dell'Eritrea (fast tank group) advancing close to a footslogged infantry column. Note how these are still in fact the early 6.5mm Fiat 14-armed CV 33 carrying the machine-gun tripod mount on the hull deck.

suffered, including three CV 33-35 tanks, two because of breakdowns. Conversely, on 15–17 April 1936 the CV 35 flamethrowers inflicted heavy losses upon Ethiopians sheltered in caves, even if the last part of the attack was carried out by the dismounted crews with hand grenades since tanks could not move closer because of the terrain. The clash on 24–25 April against the Ethiopian defence lines at Birgot, attacked by the Colonna (column) Frusci, ended successfully. In total, 143 CV 35s were deployed in Eritrea and 30 in Somaliland, with most withdrawn to Italy after the end of the war.

On 16 August 1936 the first five CV 35 tanks arrived in Vigo harbour, Spain, the first step in the Italian involvement in the Spanish Civil War officially sanctioned on 10 December of that year. The first group of Italian tanks sent to Spain was followed on 20 September by another one with ten CV 35, three of which were flamethrowers, together forming the I Raggruppamento Italo-Spagnolo carri (1st Italian–Spanish tank group). This fought with success at Navalcarnero on 21 October, facing the first tank-versus-tank combat in the history of the Italian armour at Seseña eight days later. In the engagement that saw the CV 35 against the gun-armed, Soviet-built T-26, only one Italian tank was destroyed. Shortly thereafter the unit was disbanded, and the tanks handed over to the Spanish. On 22 November 1936 the Italian military mission in Spain (Missione Militare Italiana in Spagna) was reinforced with two other tank companies and an anti-tank section; these formed, with the recovered tanks of the I Raggruppamento, three tank companies. On 8 February 1937 they supported the Italian attack against Malaga and on 17 February they formed the Raggruppamento Carri d'Assalto (assault tanks group), later on Raggruppamento Reparti Specializzati (special units group) with five companies.

Rugged terrain, along with the lack of roads, was the main hurdle to the employment of the CV 35 tanks in Ethiopia, leading in many cases to the tanks being disabled by the loss of tracks. Note the overall dark-green camouflage and the heavy layer of dust.

Italian and Spanish soldiers are celebrating on top of two CV 35 tanks by displaying a standard captured to the Republican forces. Italian tanks employed during the Spanish Civil War were camouflaged using the standard green patches on dark-sand background.

On 8–18 March the Raggruppamento supported the ill-fated Italian attack at Guadalajara, followed by the Republicans' counteroffensive. Following this defeat Italian tank units were reorganized; part now of the Comando Truppe Volontarie (volunteer troops command), the five companies formed two tank battalions as part of the Raggruppamento Celere (fast group). This eventually became in October 1937 the Raggruppamento Carristi (tank corps group), which, in the summer of 1938, was made of two tank battalions each with four companies and a support battalion. This was finally disbanded on 31 July 1939, after the victory parade at Madrid. A total of 149 CV 35 tanks were sent to Spain, 36 of which were lost either in combat or because of mechanical failures. At the end of the war some of the remaining tanks were handed over to the Spanish army.

The development of Italian armour

Experiences in Ethiopia and Spain clearly demonstrated the shortcomings of the Italian light tank; marches on rugged terrain led to frequent mechanical failures, particularly to the tracks, and the off-road range was limited to only 4–5 hours. Armour protected only against machine-gun fire, splinters and shrapnel, and not against small weapons' armour-piercing rounds and any heavy weapon, with even the 20mm gun effective at long range. Poor visibility with closed hatches, in particular with the driver's visor port at less than a metre (3 feet) from the ground, greatly limited combat capabilities along with the inadequate armament, ineffective (particularly while moving) against armoured vehicles even using armour-piercing rounds. Limited ammunition storage, insufficient traverse, absence of radios and the difficult handling of the internal crank-handle starter completed the picture. Unsurprisingly J.F.C. Fuller remarked how the Italian, German and Russian light tanks seen in action in Spain were practically useless. After the war in Ethiopia the Italian army staff

CV 35s are parading after the victorious conclusion of the war; even in spite of the actual evidence of the inferiority of the Italian light tank against the heavier, turret-equipped and gun-armed Soviet tanks such as the T-26 there were no real efforts to improve the Italian armour situation.

concluded that CV tanks could not replace infantry, but were rather to be used in large numbers in close cooperation with it.

However, the lessons from the Spanish Civil War led to no real improvement apart from an acceleration in the development of the medium tank, since experiences with enemy tank formations and captured tanks (Soviet T-26 and BT-5) left the Italians unimpressed with their performance. This was seen as the main cause for the lack of armoured breakthroughs, along with the weaknesses shown by tanks in movement warfare, prone to breakdowns and easily immobilized with ambushes, and the effectiveness of the 47/32 and 65/17 Italian guns. As a matter of fact, the Italians, like the Germans, developed not only large-size tank units (brigades), but also developed the ingenious tactic of using the CV 35 with anti-tank guns in tow; the tank acted as a bait for enemy armour, and eventually guns were used against them. That led to an overestimation of the CV 35 capabilities, either in reconnaissance or infantry support role, while its inadequacy in the tank-versus-tank combat was, if not ignored, at least temporarily set aside, waiting for the new medium tank.

While Italian tank crews started to call the CV 35 'tin of pilchards' or 'Arrigoni', after a famous brand of canned food, the tank provided the backbone of Italian armoured units until 1941 and was to remain in use until 1943, mostly against partisans in Yugoslavia. By May 1936 the Reggimento Carri Armati had formed five assault tank battalions (VIII, IX, XXIII, XXIV, XXXI), before being officially disbanded on 15 September and used to form the new fanteria carrista infantry tank corps. This now included four tank regiments: 1° Reggimento (I–III CV 35 battalions, IV Fiat 3000), 2° Reggimento (IV, V, XI CV 35 battalions, III Fiat 3000), 3° Reggimento (VI, VII CV 35 battalions, I Fiat 3000) and 4° Reggimento (VIII to X, XII CV 35 battalions, II and V Fiat 3000). By the end of 1936 the Italian army had 19 CV 35-equipped 'assault tank' battalions and five Fiat 3000 'breakthrough tank' ones.

On 1 June 1936 the 1ª Brigata motomeccanizzata (moto-mechanized brigade) was formed with the XXXI CV 35 tank battalion, one motorized Bersaglieri (light infantry) regiment and an artillery battalion. This was the last step before the final reorganization that took place on 15 July 1937 with the creation of the 1ª Brigata Corazzata

A nice study of a prewar L 3/35 tank and of its commander, unusually standing in the driver's seat, wearing the prewar uniform. Because of the lack of radio equipment the Italian tanks had to communicate using flares or coloured flags with the crews exposing from open hatches. Camouflage is overall dark sand with green mottle.

Centauro (centaur), from the Brigata motomeccanizzata with the newly formed 31° Reggimento Fanteria Carrista, and of the 2ª Brigata Corazzata Ariete (ram), formed around the 2° Reggimento Carri, renumbered 32nd in December 1938. In the same year the Corpo d'Armata Corazzato (armoured tank corps) started to take shape, followed by the development of the two brigades into armoured divisions. On 1 February 1939 the 132ª Divisione Corazzata (armoured division) Ariete, with the 32° Reggimento (II, IV, XI battalions, later on renumbered I to III; III medium tanks), was formed followed on 20 April by the 131ª Divisione Corazzata Centauro, with the 31° Reggimento (VII, VIII, X, XXXI battalions, later on renumbered I to IV). On 6 November 1939 the 133ª Divisione Corazzata Littorio did follow with the new 33° Reggimento (VI, XXII, XXIII, XXXII battalions). Their established strength was 273 officers and 7,166 other ranks, 164 tanks, 16 20mm anti-aircraft guns, eight 47/32 anti-tank guns, 24 75/27 artillery guns, and about 630 motor vehicles. The four-battalion light-tank regiment had four L 3 tanks in the regimental HQ, each battalion having 40 L 3 with this breakdown: one L 3 in the battalion HQ, three tank companies each with 13 L 3, with one L 3 in the command platoon and four in each one of the three tank platoons. One of these platoons could be equipped with the L 3/35 flamethrower.

The L 3 Semovente, a self-propelled prototype developed to carry the standard 47/32mm anti-tank gun with a crew of two. It is shown here with the gun shield removed, also revealing how crammed the space for the crew was.

At the end of 1938 the Armata Po (later 6ª Armata) was formed to control the army strategic reserve, under the command of the Corpo d'Armata Corazzato, the motorized and fast (cavalry) corps. The latter, formed by three cavalry divisions, included the only cavalry units still equipped with tanks, since all other cavalry regiments had relinquished their armoured components. In June 1940 two armoured divisions (Ariete and Littorio) were in Italy with six L 3 and two medium-tank battalions, plus three independent tank regiments with eight L 3 and one Fiat 3000 tank battalions along with three L 3 Gruppo Squadroni (cavalry battalion) of the Celeri divisions, for a grand total of 90 Fiat 3000, 820 L 3 and 72 medium tanks. The Centauro division was in Albania with four tank battalions and 132 L 3. Seven tank battalions (IX, XX, XXI, LX, LXI, LXII, LXIII) were in Libya with 324 L 3, and 63 other tanks (39 L 3, 24 medium) were in the Italian East Africa.

An L 3/35 unit parading in Rome on a rainy day, probably in October during the celebration of Mussolini's rise to power. The 1940 establishment of a light-tank battalion was 40, with each one of its three companies having 13 tanks in three platoons of four tanks each, plus a command tank.

L 3/35, UNKNOWN BATTAGLIONE CARRI L, 133ª DIVISIONE CORAZZATA LITTORIO, WESTERN ALPS JUNE 1940

The Littorio armoured division was the only Italian tank unit to take part in the short, and quite unsuccessful, attack against the French-held defences on the Western Alps in June 1940, shortly before the end of the campaign. The tank shows the typical camouflage in use in this period, with overall dark sand covered with small mottles of dark green. The L 3/35 was a rather small tank divided into three main compartments; from the rear: radiator, engine and fighting compartment. The actual size of the casemate hosting the fighting compartment was roughly the equivalent of that of both the radiator and engine compartment, with the crew of two sitting at about 50 centimetres (19.7 inches) from the ground and lacking thus a decent view of the terrain. The fighting compartment was also quite crammed, with ammunition racks on both sides and the fuel tank right behind the driver and the compartment itself divided in two with the transmission shaft and the gearbox in the middle, the latter protruding into the forward part of the fighting compartment into the front armour plates. A great use of wood, especially plywood, was made on the inside with the ammunition racks and the footboard for the crew. To start the tank from the inside the commander / machine-gunner had to fold the back of his seat and use the cranking handle on the rear panel, an excessively cumbersome procedure. Italian tanks were painted white on the inside, although most of the mechanical parts, as well as the armament, were left unpainted and only treated with lubricants.

Key

1. Radiator filler cap
2. Radiator grill
3. Engine compartment
4. SPA CV 3 four-cylinder engine
5. Hatch (machine gunner)
6. Vision slots, side
7. Ammunition rack, left side
8. Removable MG armoured plate
9. Twin 8mm Fiat 35 MGs
10. Gear handle
11. Steering levers
12. Front plate for brakes inspection
13. Sprocket wheel
14. Storage bin
15. Track
16. Rubber-tyred wheel
17. Bogie assembly
18. Headlight
19. Instrument panel
20. Driver's visor port
21. Clutch
22. Driver's seat
23. Longitudinal frame
24. Fuel tank
25. Laminated springs
26. Visor slot, rear
27. Spare wheel
28. Support wheel
29. Idle wheel (also track adjustment)
30. Exhaust
31. Fan cover, external starter for cranking handle.

6
7
8
9
10
11
12
13
14
15
16
17
18
19
20
21
22
23
24
25
26
28
28

WORLD WAR II

The opening rounds: 1940

The Italian attack against France started on 23 June 1940, almost two weeks after Italy's entry into the war on 10 June. The offensive, led across the mountain passes of the Western Alps, was supported by nine L 3 tank battalions; five of them were grouped in two *raggruppamento celere* (fast groups), while four others were with the Littorio armoured division. The I tank battalion, under command of the Trieste motorized division, attacked along the road through the Little St Bernard pass towards Saez, in the Isére valley; its march hampered by heavy snowfalls and the French artillery, it moved past road obstructions cleared by the engineers only to get entangled in a series of barbed-wire obstructions at an altitude of about 2,000 metres (1,243 miles). A second obstacle, with barbed wire and anti-tank mines, was a real hurdle causing the loss of four tanks, with two others being put out of action by the French artillery. The battalion eventually withdrew, leaving behind the damaged tanks. On 24 June a second attack across the Moncenisio pass to the Arc valley by the IV tank battalion saw the L 3 breaking through and eventually seizing a French village at the cost of two tanks, lost due to road obstacles and mines on the pass.

The first tests of war in North Africa were equally disappointing, particularly because of a fragmented use of the available L 3, split at company level into different mobile groups (*raggruppamenti*). On 15 June 1940 an Italian column, supported by two truck-borne companies of the IX light-tank battalion, was attacked by British armour while moving towards the Egyptian frontier at Sidi Omar–Capuzzo. The British forces, with armoured cars and two A 9 cruiser tanks, were able to destroy most of the column and the 12 L 3 tanks used to support it. A few days later the commander of IX battalion, Colonel D'Avanzo, was killed during a fight at Capuzzo against a mixed British unit of armoured cars, A 9 cruiser tanks and 25-pounder guns. These first clashes were quite a blow for Italian morale, especially in view of the complete unsuitability of the L 3 even against the outdated British armoured cars. Lack of armour-piercing rounds made the L 3 roughly equivalent to the British MK VI light tank, although those armed with a 12.7mm machine gun proved superior to it, but the L 3 was absolutely useless against the cruiser tanks. Furthermore its mechanical unreliability was a real hurdle, with the L 3 being slower than lorries and also unable to move more than just 5 to 10 kilometres (3 to 6 miles).

While the only two available medium-tank battalions were hastily moved to Libya, L 3 crews started to modify their tanks, equipping them with the Solothurn anti-tank rifle and the Brixia mortar, though in limited quantities. By early November 1940 the light-tank battalions only had at their disposal 32 Solothurn armed L 3, with the XXI tank battalion having apparently eight

BELOW LEFT
An L 3/35 in France, at the conclusion of the short, and quite unsuccessful, Italian offensive against France. Although specifically intended to operate in mountainous areas, the L 3 was to prove its unsuitability when moving in rugged terrain.

BELOW RIGHT
Winter training in 1939–40 in an Italian town, with a clear view of Fascist architecture. After the experiences of war in Ethiopia and Spain the light tanks were required to closely cooperate with the infantry, thus denying most of the advantages from armour and mobility. Note the crew member wearing a common winter coat.

Solothurn or 12.7mm Breda-Safat heavy machine-gun-armed L 3 in its first two companies, plus some Brixia mortar-armed ones in the third. If the armament problem was partly solved, there was no solution to the L 3's unreliability; the short-lived Italian offensive into Egypt, lasting from 8 to 17 September and halted at Sidi Barrani, was supported by 52 L 3 tanks; by 17 September 35 were lost, either because of enemy action or of breakdowns, leaving only 17 operational. Tactical use was also improved; on 29 August a Comando Carri Armati della Libia (Libya tank command) was formed, led by General Babini (commander of the *Raggruppamento Celere* in Spain). It was made of three tank *raggruppamenti* with the 1° Raggruppamento, made of the XXI, LXII and LXIII light-tank battalions and a medium-tank one, the 2° Raggruppamento made of IX, XX and LXI light-tank battalions and a medium-tank one, and the Raggruppamento Maletti made of a medium-tank company and the LX light-tank battalion. On 18 November 1940 the XXI and LX light-tank battalions, along with two medium-tank ones, formed the Brigata Corazzata Speciale (special tank or Babini tank brigade), while the other five light-tank battalions supported the infantry divisions.

The bridge-laying version of the L 3, with the 7-metre-long (23 feet) scissors bridge being automatically deployed by the crew from inside the vehicle. The bridge could also be used to cross obstacles up to 4 metres (13 feet) high.

Early in December 1940, just before the start of the British offensive (Operation *Compass*) only three light-tank battalions were in Egypt at Sidi Barrani (IX, XX and LXIII) with 125, out of a total of 270, L 3 still in running order. The British attack, supported by Matilda tanks, faced thus only ad hoc light Italian tank units with dire consequences; IX light-tank battalion was overrun at Sidi Barrani with a Libyan infantry division, with the LXIII battalion suffering the same fate at Buq Buq, and the XX battalion destroyed a few days later at the Halfaya Pass. A half-hearted counterattack led by the Brigata Corazzata Speciale with one medium tank and the LXI light-tank battalions had no results, and the British advance continued into Libya, towards Bardia. The 45,000 Italians defending it were supported by 128 tanks, mostly L 3 plus one medium (12 tanks) tank company. The 6th Australian Division, supported by the 7th Royal Tank Regiment, attacked Bardia on 3 January 1941 and, even though the Italians immobilized a few enemy tanks, early on 5 January the battle was over with an impressive result for the British and Commonwealth forces: about 40,000 prisoners, 450 guns and 127 tanks captured, including

An L 3/35 fording a river. Given the size of the tank and the lack of any real fording capability its actual limit was of 70 centimetres (27.5 inches) of water, just 10 centimetres (4 inches) more than half of its height of 1.3 metres (4.25 feet). Tactical symbol is of the 1st tank, 1st platoon, possibly 1st company (red).

An L 3 column of the Littorio armoured division crossing the Alps towards France in June 1940; the leading tank shows the tactical symbol of the commander of II battalion, its red/blue/yellow symbol denoting a three-companies battalion. Note the second tank, a flamethrower variant, with the armoured fuel trailer.

some 60–70 light and medium ones pressed into Australian service. The LXII tank battalion was lost, and only the LX light-tank battalion of the Babini tank brigade escaped, still with 24 L 3.

At this point Italian forces withdrew into Tobruk, itself strongly defended also by two medium tank battalions and the remnants of two light tank ones (XXI, LXI), with about 50 L 3. Tobruk was attacked by Australian forces on 21 January 1941, and the following day the Italians surrendered, thus opening the way to the last leap of O'Connor's offensive: the drive into the desert of Cyrenaica to Agedabia. The Babini tank brigade did try to check the British advance at El Mechili, but its medium and light tanks were no match for the enemy cruiser and the Matilda tanks. After the clash the LX tank battalion withdrew west along with the remnants of the LXI, together still with some 25 L 3 in running order, seven of which were armed with the Solothurn AT rifle or the 12.7 MG. Both battalions were eventually destroyed at Beda Fomm on 5–7 February 1941.

The last round in North Africa and the other fronts

In February 1941, when the first German units under the command of General Rommel started to arrive in Libya, there were only 46 L 3 still available with the IV and V light-tank battalions, hurriedly sent from Italy in December 1940. Between 24 January and 26 February 1941 the whole of the Ariete armoured division followed, with its three light-tank battalions (I–III, followed by the VII, equipped with medium tanks), and a total of 93 machine-gun-armed and 24 flamethrower L 3. This measure was dictated by necessity, and by the lack of any other medium-tank battalion. Thus the L 3 continued to fight in North Africa until late 1941, in spite of the eventual creation of a new medium-tank-equipped 32° Reggimento Carri in August 1941.

L 3/35 in North Africa 1940–41. In spite of its obsolescence the tankette saw widespread use until late 1941 in North Africa and until 1943 in the Balkans, with the Ariete armoured division arriving in Libya in February 1941 still equipped with them. Note the European camouflage under a layer of dust and sand.

ABOVE LEFT
A front view of an L 3/35 in North Africa; note the protection covers for the headlights and machine guns, the machine-gun top armour pulled down and how, in spite of the opened visor port, the driver needed to expose his head to have a good view of the terrain.

ABOVE RIGHT
The third platoon of an unknown unit parading at the conclusion of a training session in Libya. Note the crew members, all wearing the standard Italian tank suit made of a double-breasted leather jacket, and the very small size of the tankette compared to the crew.

Unsurprisingly, even though the Ariete took part in Rommel's first offensive in April 1941, its tanks saw little or no action at all. On this occasion the L 3 would still enjoy some advantage since, being mostly truck-borne, it suffered less from the wear and tear that afflicted the medium tanks during the march to Tobruk. When Tobruk was surrounded by the Axis forces the Ariete was part of the attacks led against the Australian-held fortress; the first on 16–17 April, with about 50 L 3 (including flamethrowers) and ten medium tanks, suffering heavy losses. The second attack on 30 April–4 May was led by three L 3 companies supported by three medium tanks, plus the German Panzer. This too ended in a failure, and at the end of June the three light-tank battalions of the Ariete were considered no longer battleworthy either because of losses or mechanical breakdowns (a special request was made to replace all their engines). Only in August the division recovered 108 L 3, which, along with those of the IV and V battalions, were deployed around Tobruk, supporting the Italian infantry, once more in an *ad hoc* way (15 each to two divisions, 14 and 25 to another two, leaving 64 with the Ariete and 15 with XX Corps HQ). Furthermore, they were employed in pairs or platoons to support infantry actions, possibly a suitable use for the L 3, but involving great attrition for men and machines. Worth noting, only some of these L 3 were equipped with the Solothurn anti-tank rifle.

On 15 November 1941 there were still 187 L 3 in North Africa, eventually to get involved in 8th Army's attack (Operation *Crusader*) that started on the 18th with the aim of rescuing Tobruk. Employed again in a piecemeal way they suffered heavy losses fighting against modern tanks, even though (if wisely led) they still possessed a certain degree of effectiveness. On 23 November a mixed unit with companies from IV and V battalion under command of the Trento division attacked a British column, closing down to it before being forced to withdraw under artillery fire. Of the 29 L 3 that took part in this action 25 made their way back. Another attack led by the same unit on 29 November in the Bir Garsa area was moderately successful, although ten of the 14 L 3 taking part in it were hit and four were lost. The last L 3 tank of the Trento division saw action on 3 December. On 19 November the I and II battalions of Ariete's 32nd regiment fought at Bir el Gubi against the 22nd British Armoured Brigade, and about a month later, following the withdrawal to the Gazala line, the Ariete had practically lost all of its L 3, mostly because of mechanical breakdowns. The last L 3 that saw action were those of the 3rd company, IV battalion, deployed at the Halfaya where the Axis forces had been surrounded and eventually surrendered on 17 January 1942. At this time there were no more L 3 in running order in North Africa.

ABOVE LEFT
A Semovente L 40 disembarked during the exercises for the planned invasion of Malta. The vehicle is in overall sand with the tactical symbol of 2nd platoon painted on the hull side and the plate painted on the front plate. Note the crew, wearing the standard tank crew overalls and crash helmets.

ABOVE RIGHT
Another example of a Semovente L 40 in Tunisia in 1942–43; this is an intermediate version of the self-propelled gun, with the access hatch on the left side of the hull welded. A subsequent version had the access hatch removed.

On 28 October 1940 the ill-fated Italian attack against Greece started, with the Centauro division spearheading it with 170 L 3, including 37 flamethrowers; the division advanced slowly to Kalibaki, losing 14 of its tanks while attacking it. After the Greek counterattack in November–December, the Centauro was pulled out of the line and reinforced with a medium-tank battalion, while transferring its I and III battalions to other units. Its 31° Reggimento was back again to the front in January 1941, fighting in the Klisura area without success; another attack, led on 19 March in the mountain area of Monastir, ended again in a failure with the loss of two out of five tanks. Following the German attack against Greece and Yugoslavia in April 1941 the Centauro was redeployed to the Yugoslav border in Macedonia. After repulsing a half-hearted counterattack, it eventually advanced into Yugoslavia only to face anti-tank gun positions, which cost the loss of 11 L 3 and five other damaged. Better fate was met by the Littorio, which attacked Yugoslavia from the north, eventually establishing contact with the Italian forces advancing from Albania, its 33° Reggimento (with 117 L 3 and five medium tanks) advancing for more than 1,000 kilometres (621 miles) facing almost no opposition.

In June 1941 the CSIR (Corpo di Spedizione Italiano in Russia, Italian expedition corps to Russia) was sent to the Eastern Front, its only tank unit being the cavalry III Gruppo Squadroni San Giorgio, part of the 3rd celere (cavalry) division with about 60 L 3. It fought in southern Ukraine facing no Soviet tanks, until reaching the Dneiper river in September and losing three tanks in the crossing. Early in October there still were some 40 L 3 in running order, reduced to a dozen in December after an advance of about 1,400 kilometres (870 miles). Eventually tank crews were sent back to Italy to re-equip with the L 6/40, while an Italian army was being transferred to the Eastern Front.

The RECo and the L 6 tank

Already in early 1941 it was clear how light tanks were quite useless in combat, although they still retained a use in reconnaissance. The unsuitability of the outdated L 3 and the scarce availability of the AB 40-41 armoured cars delayed the development of Italian reconnaissance units to early 1942, when a new mechanization of cavalry was started. Cavalry regiments, and a single Bersaglieri (light infantry) one were transformed in RECo, or Raggruppamento Esplorante Corazzato (armoured reconnaissance group), intended to provide armoured and motorized divisions with a mixed armoured reconnaissance unit.

A view of the top of a Semovente L 40 negotiating mud in Tunisia in 1942–43; this view gives an idea of the crammed space of the fighting compartment with the pilot on the right, the loader immediately behind him and the gunner/commander on the left.

Its 1942 establishment included an HQ squadron and two Gruppo esplorante corazzato (armoured reconnaissance groups), the first equipped with one armoured car and two L 6/40 squadrons, the second with one L 40 self-propelled gun, one anti-aircraft and one motorcycle-mounted squadron.

The first to be formed was the 18° RECo Bersaglieri (18th Bersaglieri regiment) on 1 February 1942, soon split into three different divisions: its VIII battalion was attached to the motorized Trieste and the XXII to the Centauro armoured division, both in North Africa, while the LXVII went to the 3ª celere division on the Eastern Front. The 15° RECo Cavalleggeri di Lodi was formed on 15 February 1942; attached to the Centauro armoured division it was sent to North Africa in September–November 1942, but it lost its self-propelled L 40 squadron en route and was left with its two L 6/40 squadrons that fought in Tunisia until May 1943 along with the Centauro. The last to be formed, on 15 July 1942, was the 8° RECo Lancieri di Montebello; it had no L 6/40 tank squadrons, although its second Gruppo esplorante corazzato had two L 40 self-propelled gun squadrons. Attached to the rebuilt Ariete armoured division it fought in Rome against the Germans in the days following the Italian surrender of 8 September 1943.

Other cavalry units were mechanized, even if to a limited extent with only six out of 18 cavalry regiments eventually transformed. Units equipped with both the L 6/40 tanks and the L 40 self-propelled guns were in 1942 the III Gruppo Corazzato (armoured group) of the Nizza Cavalleria regiment (L 6/40), attached in June 1942 to the Ariete division. It fought at El Alamein and in Tunisia. The III Gruppo Squadroni Lancieri di Novara was sent to North Africa in September–October 1942 and attached to the Littorio armoured division. It fought at El Alamein and was disbanded after the loss of all its tanks, primarily due to mechanical breakdowns. Other units fought in the Balkans or on the Eastern Front; mostly

Two L 3/35 move on a dusty road on the Eastern Front in 1941; some 60 of them, part of the III Gruppo Squadroni San Giorgio (armoured cavalry battalion) of the 3rd cavalry division, were sent along with the Italian expeditionary corps, fighting until early 1942.

equipped with L 40 self-propelled guns, plus some L 6/40 tanks, the IV Gruppo Corazzato of the Cavalleggeri di Monferrato regiment was employed in Yugoslavia, as was the III and IV Gruppo Corazzato of the Cavalleggeri di Alessandria regiment, whose L 40 self-propelled guns of the XIII Gruppo Squadroni went to the Eastern Front along with the LXVII Bersaglieri. A few L 6/40 also equipped other cavalry regiments, such as the Piemonte Cavalleria and the Cavalleggeri Guide, as well as the 'I Gruppo Squadroni San Giusto' of the 1ª celere (cavalry) division. The L 40 self-propelled gun also equipped a certain number of anti-tank and self-propelled battalions (*battaglioni controcarri* and *semoventi*), mostly to see action in Tunisia and in Sicily in 1943; these included (actual numbering was in Roman) the Battaglioni controcarri 101 (Tunisia), 102 to 104, and 867 (Sicily), and the Battaglioni semoventi 1 (Tunisia), 4 (Sicily), 12 (Tunisia), 133 (Sicily), 136 (Tunisia) and 230 (Sicily).

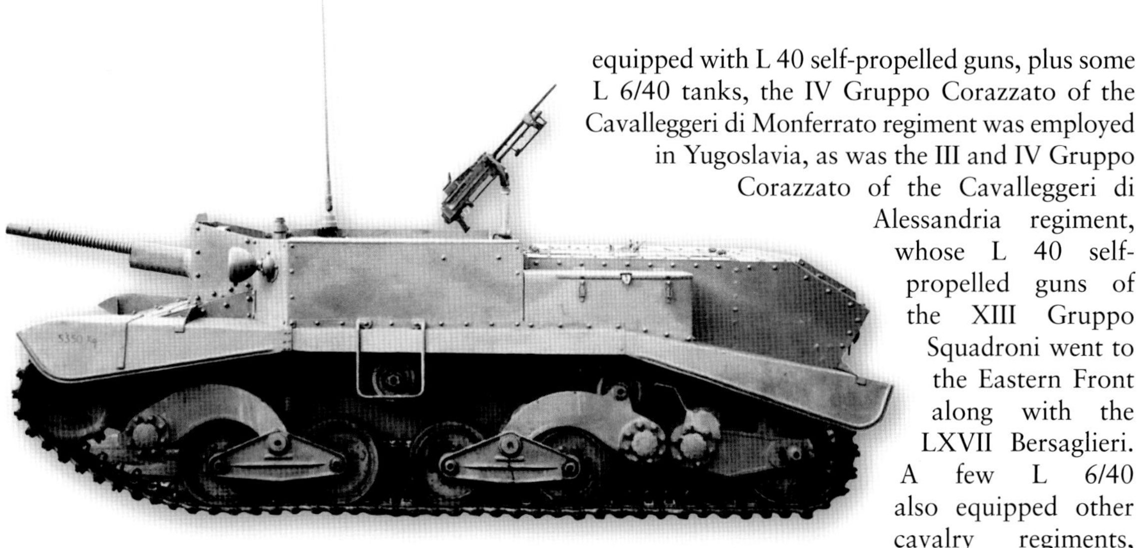

The Cingoletta Ansaldo L 6 was the prototype of a caterpillar tractor based on the L 6 chassis, with the whole upper portion of the hull removed and the front hull armour plates reshaped to accommodate a 13.2mm Breda 31 machine gun, along with an 8mm Breda 38 in an anti-aircraft mount.

Actual employment was limited in spite of the number of units formed; only 42 L 6/40 tanks were in North Africa by 19 October, with both the III Gruppo Novara and the 15° RECo Lodi. An estimate gives a total of 77 L 6/40 and about 80 L 40 self-propelled guns employed up to May 1943. Sixty L 6/40 tanks of the LXVII Bersaglieri battalion and 19 L 40 self-propelled guns of the XIII Gruppo Squadroni Cavalleggeri di Alessandria were on the Eastern Front from the summer of 1942, with the ARMIR (Armata Italiana in Russia, Italian army in Russia), soon to suffer from lack of adequate fuel and lubricants in the Russian winter. During the retreat followed the Soviet offensive started on 11 December 1942, those still in running order were soon lost, mostly because of mechanical breakdowns or simple lack of fuel. By September 1943 some 70 L 6/40 tanks and 90 L 40 self-propelled guns were still available in Italy.

F

L 3/35, UNKNOWN BATTAGLIONE CARRI L, 132ª DIVISIONE CORAZZATA ARIETE, LIBYA 1941

The last L 3/35 production series, built in 1938, had the main armament replaced with two 8mm Breda 38 machine guns that gave an improved traverse over the old 8mm Fiat 35; the Breda, with their shorter barrels, could be traversed 28° in both directions as opposed to the Fiat, which only had 24° traverse (Breda also had a vertical traverse of 36° against the 27° of the Fiat). Since in the same year some L 3/35 were modified into L 3/38 with the new suspensions applied, it is more common to see the L 3/38 armed with the Breda, although even L 3/35 tanks had them. Ariete armoured division tanks arrived in Libya in February 1941 with the old standard overall dark-green camouflage and were repainted sand by their crews, often covering the tactical symbols as in this case. Sometimes the hull roof and engine deck were not repainted to preserve the white aerial recognition disc; this was usually painted on the engine deck but there were variations: the 3rd Reggimento Carri only had a half disc while the 4th used a cross painted on the left hatch, and the LXI L tanks battalion used a white disc on the right hatch.

Another, earlier prototype of the Cingoletta Ansaldo L 6, this time armed with an 8mm Breda 38 machine gun in the hull mount. This vehicle was intended for use as an ammunition and personnel carrier, but the AS 37 Sahariana truck was eventually preferred to it.

Light tanks in German service

Although a grand total of more than 340 L 3, L 6/40 tanks and semoventi L 40 were seized by the Germans after the Italian surrender in September 1943, these only saw limited use and production under German control in 1943-45 mainly focused on the semovente L 40 (120 produced), with only 17 L 6/40 tanks and some other 17 L 3 ones produced (the latter probably rebuilt from recovered vehicles). Most of the L 3 tanks went to second line formations or organizations, particularly police units or the Organization Todt, being mostly used as tractors (like the semovente L 40) or even as armoured dugouts. The only units equipped with them were, in Italy, the Panzer Ausbildung Abteilung Süd (a training tank battalion, which also had L 6/40 tanks and semoventi L 40) and the Panzer Abteilung Adria (Adriatic tank battalion), fighting along the Italian Gruppo Squadroni Corazzati 'San Giusto' against Yugoslav partisan on the eastern border. L 3 tanks, along with the L 6/40 ones and the semovente L 40 also equipped in the Balkans the three Croatian infantry divisions fighting under German control (369th, 373rd, 392nd), and the 7th SS Gebirgs Division 'Prinz Eugen'. Also in the Balkans the following German units were equipped with semoventi L 40: 117th and 118th Jäger divisions, 181st, 264th and 297th infantry divisions, the 4th SS Polizei Division, while the Panzer Kompanie z.b.V. 12 (later Abteilung; a Panzer company for special purposes upgraded early 1944 to a battalion) and the SS Panzer Abteilung 105 had both L 6/40 tanks and semoventi L 40. Light tanks and semoventi saw a much more limited use in Italy, equipping the 114th Jäger, 305th and 356th infantry, plus the 11th Luftwaffe Feld divisions (all only with the semoventi L 40), and the Heeres Schwere Panzerjäger Abteilung 590 (army heavy anti-tank battalion, with L 6/40 tanks and semoventi L 40 mostly used as tractors). Six L 6/40 tanks equipped each one of the police units both in Italy and in the Balkans, and some L 3 tanks were even employed on the Western Front in 1944.

In 1942 the L 6/40 replaced the L 3 on the Eastern Front with the 3rd cavalry division, this time equipping the LXVII Bersaglieri battalion, part of the 18th Bersaglieri regiment that in 1942 was transformed in an armoured reconnaissance unit. The tactical symbol denotes the 2nd tank of the 5th platoon, possibly 2nd company.

The Germans complained that Italian light tanks, apart from being mostly obsolete, lacked reliability, armour and adequate guns, all to worsen with time. Lack of spare parts required constant maintenance and eventual cannibalization of tanks no longer in running order, difficulties with the supplies of ammunition (particularly for the units in the Balkans) had the Italian weapons being adapted for use with the German ammunition or even replaced, which also accounts for the widespread use of the light tanks as tractors or prime movers, and in many cases field modifications were needed to improve some of their deficiencies. For example, semoventi L 40 had a machine gun mounted on the superstructure (which in some cases had a protection added on the top), and extra boxes added on the hull. Even when used against the partisans, the light tanks and semovente only operated in small groups, with the vehicles providing each other fire support during marches and combat. However, attrition took a heavy toll as the situation of the Panzer Ausbildung Abteilung Süd (which was not a combat unit) shows; in December 1944 it still had seven L 3, three L 6 and seven semoventi or command L 40 in its inventory, none of which were still available by February 1945.

CAMOUFLAGE AND MARKINGS

The first camouflage pattern introduced with the Fiat 3000 was an overall sand colour with large irregular green and reddish-brown blotches. With the CV 33 tank the standard overall dark grey-green camouflage colour, already in use with other vehicles, was adopted. A new camouflage scheme was then established with grey-green patches added to the earth-brown/dark-sand basic colour, although brown patches could be added to the grey-green base. The first tanks sent to Libya were painted overall yellowish-green, a colour retained during the Italian–Ethiopian war. During the Spanish Civil War the Italian tanks retained the standard European camouflage of dark sand with dark-green patches. From 1937 to 1939 all the AFVs produced by Ansaldo-Fiat were painted overall sand with small green and red-brown stripes, but in 1939 the old camouflage schemes were reintroduced. Light tanks sent to Libya in the summer of 1940 retained the standard camouflage scheme, unsuitable for the area, and crews generally repainted them with sand. From March 1941 a new camouflage scheme – overall dark sand – was introduced for North Africa, and in November Ansaldo was ordered to paint all the new AFVs in the standard overall dark-sand scheme. Tanks in Europe could alter the basic camouflage with stripes or patches, whatever was most suitable. Following the end of the war in North Africa in May 1943 a new European camouflage scheme was adopted, with green and brown stripes or patches applied on the overall dark sand, but in the summer of 1943 some AFVs were still painted overall grey-green, sometimes with the green and brown camouflage added.

BELOW TOP
Different types of tactical symbols were used by the CV 35 tanks during the Spanish Civil War; the ones used during the last stage of the war (from 1937) were made of half circles painted in different colours or combinations to denote the company, with the tank number painted inside.

BELOW BOTTOM
A foliage-camouflaged Semovente L 40 in 1943, also carrying a noticeable amount of extra equipment on the engine deck. These self-propelled guns equipped both the armoured reconnaissance units (RECo) and the anti-tank gun battalions.

An L 3/35 restored and preserved in an Italian army barrack, painted overall sand with the insignia of the Ariete (ram) armoured division on the side and the red/blue pennant of the Italian tank troops. The pulled-down armoured plate on the upper part of the gun mount is clearly visible. The engine deck was altered post-war to fit a new engine and allow the tank to parade.

Italian tank markings used at first geometric figures in different colours, to denote either the tank or the squadron/company in order of seniority (red, white, orange, blue, green, black). Command tanks had either a circle or a triangle, in different positions, while other tanks had a series of stripes (up to three), which, in different positions, denoted the platoon and the number of the tank in it. From 1928 these markings were reduced to the outline, until a new scheme was introduced in 1938. This, made of rectangles, introduced a new colour scheme (red, blue, yellow, green) to denote companies, while the platoon number was shown by a series of white stripes, one to four, painted inside the rectangle. The individual tank number was painted above these rectangles. Battalion command tanks had a red/blue (two companies battalion) or red/blue/yellow rectangle (three companies battalion), with the HQ squadron ones having a black rectangle. White rectangles with black stripes were used by the regimental HQ.

SURVIVING VEHICLES

Fiat 3000 and CV 29 apart, several Italian light tanks are still preserved (a few in running order) all around the world; there are 22 L 3 tanks in Italy, including a flamethrower. These are mostly in barracks, apart from the following: two at the Museo della Fanteria (Rome), two (including the flamethrower) at the Museo de Henriquez (Trieste), one at the Museo della Motorizzazione Militare (Rome). Some other 18 are preserved abroad, notably a flamethrower at Bovington Tank Museum (UK), still with its trailer. Three L 6/40 tanks are preserved, one in an Italian barracks (Solbiate Olona, Varese), one at the Kubinka Musem (Russia) and one at the Gjirokastër Museum (Albania). A single Semovente L 40, a company command version, is preserved at the Aberdeen Proving Ground (Maryland, USA).

G

SEMOVENTE L 40, UNKNOWN BATTAGLIONE CONTROCARRI, TUNISIA 1943

Built on the chassis of the L 6/40 tank, the self-propelled gun Semovente L 40 was an unsatisfactory solution, like the tank it was based upon. With no improved performances over the L 6/40, the Semovente L 40 was armed with the standard Italian 47/32 anti-tank gun, which, by the standards of 1942–43, was already largely outdated and no longer effective against most enemy tanks. Furthermore, the crammed space inside the fighting compartment and the reduced crew of three limited its actual capabilities on the battlefield. Used to equip the SP gun companies of the RECo, the Semovente L 40 also formed several *battaglioni controcarri* (anti-tank battalions) employed in Tunisia and Sicily against the Allies. In many cases the Semovente L 40 in Tunisia, all camouflaged overall sand, had either no tactical symbols at all or very small ones. Extensive use of foliage seems to have been the preferred way to add further camouflage to these vehicles. Crews of the Semovente with the *battaglioni controcarri* could wear either tank crews' overalls and leather jackets or the standard uniforms of the Italian soldiers.

SPECIFICATIONS

L 3/35	
Weight	3.2 tons
Dimensions Length Width Height	 3.15 metres 1.5 metres 1.3 metres
Armour Front Sides/rear Floor/Roof	 13.5/15mm * 8.5/9mm * 6mm
Powerplant	SPA CV 3-005 engine, 43hp at 2,400rpm
Speed Max (road) Off-road	 42kph 15kph
Range Road Off-Road	 150km 6 hours
Armament	Two 8mm Fiat 35 MG 2,170 rounds
Ground clearance	32cm
Fording depth	70cm
Trench crossing	1.45 metres
Vertical obstacle	60cm
Climbing ability	45°
* earlier and later models	

	L 6/40	Semovente L 40 (differences)
Weight	6.8 tons	6.5 tons
Dimensions Length Width Height	 3.82 metres 1.86 metres 2.17 metres	 1.69 metres
Armour Front Sides/rear Floor/Roof	 30/40 (turret) mm 15mm 6mm	 30mm
Powerplant	SPA 18 VT engine, 68hp at 2,500rpm	
Speed Max (road) Off-road	 42kph 25kph	
Range Road Off-Road	 200km 10 hours (85km)	
Armament	One 20mm Breda 35 (280, later 312 rounds); One 8mm Breda 38 MG (1,056, later 1,560 rounds)	One 47mm L 32 AT gun (70 rounds)
Ground clearance	40cm	
Fording depth	80cm	
Trench crossing	1.70 metres	
Vertical obstacle	80cm	
Climbing ability	70°	

BIBLIOGRAPHY

'L'armamento italiano nella 2ª guerra mondiale. Fronte terra. Vol. 1: Carri armati in servizio fra le due guerre', Rome, Bizzarri (1972)

'L'armamento italiano nella 2ª guerra mondiale. Fronte terra. Vol. 2/1: Carri armati. Carri leggeri, carro veloce 33-35, evoluzione del mezzo', Rome, Bizzarri (1973)

'L'armamento italiano nella 2ª guerra mondiale. Fronte terra. Vol. 2/II: Carri armati. Carri leggeri, carro veloce 33-35, le operazioni belliche', Rome, Bizzarri (1973)

'L'armamento italiano nella 2ª guerra mondiale. Fronte terra. Vol. 2/III: Carri armati. Carri leggeri, L6/40 sviluppo ed operazioni', Rome, Bizzarri (1974)

Ceva, Lucio and Curami, Andrea, 'La meccanizzazione dell'esercito fino al 1943' (Rome, Stato Maggiore Esercito – Ufficio Storico, 1989)

Falessi, Cesare and Pafi, Benedetto, 'Veicoli da combattimento dell'esercito italiano dal 1939 al 1945', Interconair, Bologna (1976)

Pignato, Nicola, 'Il carro veloce Ansaldo. Un'icona degli anni Trenta', Storia Militare, Parma (2004)

Pignato, Nicola, 'I mezzi blindo-corazzati italiani 1923–1943. Dal reparto carri armati al corpo d'armata corazzato', Storia Militare, Parma (2005)

Bruschi, Alessandro and Guglielmi, Daniele, 'Light tank. Carro leggero L3-33/35/38 and L6/semovente L40' (Genua, Pignato, Nicola–Cappellano, Filippo, 'Gli autoveicoli da combattimento dell'esercito italiano. Vol. I: Dalle origini fino al 1939', SME-US, Rome (2002)

Pignato, Nicola and Cappellano, Filippo, 'Gli autoveicoli da combattimento dell'esercito italiano. Vol. II: 1940–1945', SME-US, Rome (2002)

Pignato, Nicola, 'I mezzi corazzati italiani 1939–1945', Storia Militare, Parma (1996)

Talillo, Andrea e Antonio and Guglielmi, Daniele, 'Carro L3. Carri veloci, carri leggeri, derivati', Gruppo Modellistica Trentino, Trento (2004)

Talillo, Andrea e Antonio and Guglielmi, Daniele, 'Carro L6. Carri leggeri, semoventi, derivati' (Gruppo Modellistica Trentino, Trento (2007)

Walker, Ian W., *Iron Hulls, Iron Hearts*, Crowood Press, Ramsbury, Wiltshire (2003)

Another sample of a preserved L 3/35 tank at the army barrack of Cordenons, this time a variant with internal riveting and different vision slots. The insignia painted on the upper hull side refers to the Ariete division in North Africa, but was not used during the war.

INDEX

Page numbers shown in **bold** refer to illustrations